THE

INSTAGRAM

INFLUENCERS

*How to Upgrade Your Marketing by Using
the Most Profitable Social Media Creators*

by **HERMAN J. ALLAN**

1

Congratulation on purchase this book and thank You for doing so.

Please enjoy*!*

© Copyright 2021 by **HERMAN J. ALLAN**

Table of Contents

3

Influencer Marketing Defined?

Influencer marketing is a form of joint effort. A business collaborates with a persuasive individual to promote something. It could be a product, administration, or campaign. Celebrity supports were the first form of influencer marketing. Yet, in today's computerized world, social content makers with niche audiences can regularly offer more an incentive to brands. These people have committed and drawn in groups of followers via web-based networking media. They are referred to just as "web based life influencers." More than 66% of North American retailers utilize some form of influencer marketing. What's more, practically 50% of US and UK computerized advertisers spend in any event 10% of their marketing correspondence budget on influencer marketing.

Not persuaded influencer marketing can lead to genuine business results? A study found that 34% of every day U.S. Instagram clients purchased something in light of the fact that a blogger or influencer suggested it. Instagram is the platform of decision for social influencers. 89% of advertisers distinguish it as one of the most significant channels for influencer marketing.

About 33% of the influencer content on Instagram appears in Stories. This number will probably grow this year. The swipe-up feature to link out from Instagram Stories is presently accessible to accounts with only 10,000 followers. This makes Stories a great spot to share and link to brand content. Yet, don't disregard different platforms. About a fourth of day by day Facebook clients have made a buy based on a blogger or influencer suggestion. So have 29% of day by day Twitter clients.

How to find the right social media influencer in 8 easy steps

There are in excess of 500,000 dynamic influencers on Instagram alone. That means you have numerous potential open doors for influencer joint effort. It additionally means you need to place in the work to find the privilege influencer. Advertisers' trust in their capacity to find the privilege influencer changes generally by nation. In China, 81% of marketing experts are certain they can find effective influencers. In the United States, just 39% of advertisers feel a similar way.

Here are 8 key approaches to find and associate with the privilege influencer for your campaign.

1. *THINK ABOUT THE THREE RS OF INFLUENCE*

Influence is made up of three parts:
- Relevance
- Reach
- Resonance

Relevance

An applicable influencer shares content important to your business and industry. They have to have an audience that lines up with your objective market. For instance, Intrepid Travel worked with a group of vegetarian influencers to dispatch its new veggie lover visits. The influencers' had an exceptionally significant audience that the company accessed in a drawing in and authentic way. Erin Ireland is an energetic veggie lover advocate. Her Instagram post about how the visit opened up movement for her in India as a vegetarian increased in excess of 5,700 preferences.

Reach

Reach is the quantity of people you might reach through the influencer's devotee base.

Resonance

This is the potential degree of engagement the influencer can create with an audience pertinent to your brand. Greater isn't in every case better. A colossal adherent tally is insignificant if those followers aren't keen on your offer. What's more, a littler supporter check can be ground-breaking if it's a niche zone. Niche influencers can have exceptionally devoted and connected with followers. Tap-influence found that engagement rates are frequently higher for "micro-influencers." Micro-influencers have 5,000 to 25,000 followers. 30% of North American retailers presently work with micro-influencers. The most recent improvement is the development of nano-influencers. These influencers can have as not many as 1,000 followers, yet their statement is gold to their committed fans.

2. BE SURE OF WHO YOU'RE ATTEMPTING TO INFLUENCE

Your influencer campaign can't be everything to all people. A practical strategy anticipates that you should address the ideal people using the right tools. (Likewise, for this circumstance, the benefit influencers).The introductory advance is to describe who your audience will be for this particular campaign. Making audience personas is a great technique to make sure you understand who you're attempting to reach. At the point when you've done that, create a planning arrangement of influencer personas. This will help you with understanding the attributes you're searching for in your influencers.

3. SEARCH FOR ENGAGEMENT AND TRUST WITH THE RIGHT AUDIENCE

The key is trust. Your audience must trust and respect the evaluation of the influencers you partner with. Without the trust portion, any results will be superficial. You'll fight to see a significant business influence from your undertakings. How might you tell if your potential influencer is trusted? Engagement. You have to see a lot of viewpoints, likes, comments, and offers. In particular, you have to see these from the definite adherent areas you're attempting to reach. A not too bad engagement rate additionally means a dedicated after, instead of an inflated adherent check fortified by bots and coercion accounts.

4. GO FOR A RELIABLE LOOK, FEEL, TONE, AND QUALITIES

You have to find somebody who's creating content with a look and feel that supplements your own. The tone should likewise be appropriate for the manner in which you need to introduce your brand to potential customers. This will guarantee things don't feel disconnected in either party's internet based life posts.

5. WATCH OUT FOR SPONSORSHIP IMMERSION

Investigate the post of your potential influencers from time to time. How regularly would they say they are sharing sponsored content? If they're already hitting followers with huge amounts of paid posts, their engagement rate may not last. Search for a lot of natural, non-paid content to keep followers intrigued, excited, and locked in. YouTube influencer Laura Reid prescribes just having one in each five or 10 posts sponsored. Remember this when considering what you'll ask the influencer to post, also. Requesting an excessive number of posts in a short timeframe will make your offer hard for the influencer to acknowledge, regardless of whether it accompanies an enormous paycheck.

6. RESEARCH AND LEARN

Popular influencers get lots of offers. At the point when you first approach an influencer, you'll have to show that you've placed in the time to learn what they do. Get to recognizes what their channels are about and who their audience is. Shockingly better, start your approach gradually by collaborating naturally with your objective influencer's posts. Like their content. Remark when appropriate. Be appreciative, not salesly.

7. *PLAN YOUR BUDGET*

Influencers with broad reach appropriately hope to be paid for their work. Free product may work with nano-influencers, yet a bigger influencer campaign requires a budget. Consider what sort of payment structure makes the most sense for your goals. Be that as it may, be happy to think about the influencer's needs, as well. For instance, an affiliate or commission structure may be a choice instead of a flat fee, or to lessen the flat fee. We've sketched out the different payment models in our post on the most proficient method to pay Instagram influencers. Remember that micro-influencers and nano-influencers will have increasingly adaptable payment terms.

8. *REACH OUT PERSONALLY, AND PRIVATELY*

An immediate message is a great spot to start. In the event that you can find an email address, attempt that as well. However, don't send a mass email or conventional DM. It might take somewhat longer to compose an individual message to each influencer. In any case, it will show you're not kidding about a potential partnership. This will thusly build your chances of striking an arrangement.

How to Get Instagram Sponsorship for Making Money

When you clock 1000 plus followers on Instagram and on the look for sponsorship in Instagram, do you know how to proceed? If the uncertainty factor in Instagram sponsorship is weighing heavily on your heart, then don't fret. It is likely to get Instagram sponsorship for small accounts and garner more exposure in your niche market by making excellent and engaging videos. In this section, we are going to introduce the ways that would help you get sponsorship in Instagram and earn more revenues.

Part1: Is it possible to find Instagram sponsorship for small accounts

Part2: How to get Instagram sponsorship

Gone are the days when brands only looked for extremely popular influencers with a trailing list of followers. Under their Instagram sponsorship program now brands look for micro-influencers within the exact niche. Because they shed less bucks to reach the right audience in a target demographics. Micro-influencers are low-budget but high rewards aspects for any business. Usually Instagram popular accounts are less interactive, when compared to average Instagram accounts from the ROI point of view. There is less engagement for accounts having millions of followers. When you have a limited number of followers, your response will be instant and the engagement will be better. Instagram sponsored posts nowadays come with brand + influencer collaborations. This is an integral part for your business to flourish in Instagram.

PART 2: HOW TO GET INSTAGRAM SPONSORSHIP

1. Know your audience well
Understanding what content on your Instagram posts satisfies your audience isn't sufficient. You have to dive further and become acquainted with

how to make your posts associate with them better with your product or services. Step by step instructions to bring out their feelings based on their age range, area, sexual orientation conveyance, and how did your post performed. Instagram sponsorship would turn out to be easy, when you will obviously clarify brands about your followers' needs and likes. Realizing that you have better understanding about the niche and sort of audience will score more atta boy with the brands ready to collaborate with you.

2. Use Instagram sponsorship apps

There are various apps that assist you with working together with advertisers and influencers to promote your brand. Influencer platforms advance your name in the influencer shopping commercial center, accordingly the brand sponsorships crosswise over significant online networking platforms start seeing you. GOsnap is one of the best assistance with leading influencers on Instagram, Twitter, and YouTube. On the off chance that you get a chance, don't stop for a second to collaborate with your favorite brands for paid Instagram sponsorship. GOsnap offers you easy signup with your internet based life account, no agreements to sign, paid sponsorship bargains directly at your versatile, join campaigns that you love and so forth in addition, share visit individual posts via web-based networking media with followers and acquire more bucks through ledger or PayPal.

3. Contact the brand you like
Connect with your favorite brands decisively to pitch your thought. You can likewise label their brand name, account or handle with your post. With an influencer's content thought, you get significant and authentic sponsorship for your Instagram posts.

4. Improve engagement rate.
Expanded engagement on your Instagram posts means better change to get featured on the Instagram Explore page. This page on Instagram permits influencers reach people who are not their followers. A snappy viral status over yonder could be the what tops off an already good thing for you. With the correct content and adhering to the fundamental Instagram rules would soar your chances of better presentation. Peruse your adherent's page and remark on their posts. Join Instagram remarks units for better informing with your followers to upgrade the engagement.

5. Be genuine and authentic

Instagram sponsorship programs expect you to be authentic and reasonable. Continuously make sure to remain consistent with your followers and post content that is speaking to your brand identity. While working together with brands and influencers on Instagram acquires more incomes. Never, disregard the way that your followers are the purpose for your growth. Instead of clustering your account with posts that are unmistakable difference to your brand identity would cost you losing your followers, pick the ones that hold your visual identity. While you give a whoop to different brands, don't lose your brand's voice by any stretch of the imagination.

6. Don't neglect to affiliate

Instagram sponsorship for little accounts is clearly going to assist you with pushing forward. Along with that, be sure to affiliate with others for upgrading the sales of your brand's products or services. An affiliate is essentially engaged at improving the sales of brands partnering with them for a commissions. Though influencers are essentially associated with making brand awareness. There is an identifiable link or certain promotion code that followers can click for really purchasing your administration/product. As links in Instagram are permitted distinctly in the bio, you need to think of one as product on the double for applying affiliate links. Making promotion codes is a superior substitute to lace them with your posts. However, Instagram is permitting links in Instagram Stories now.

Here are some famous affiliate platforms with online shippers that you can investigate – ClickBank, RewardStyle, and Amazon's Affiliate Program are not many of them. Utilize other marketing channels and your website to reinforce the affiliate program.

Guide to Creating Instagram Ads

Instagram advertising is strategy for paying to post sponsored content on the Instagram platform to reach a bigger and more focused on audience. While there are many reasons a business or individual may choose to advertise, Instagram advertising is frequently used to grow brand introduction, website traffic, generate new leads, and move current leads down the pipe (and hopefully towards converting).Since Instagram is such a visual platform, content ads are not a thing here. Or maybe you need a picture, set of pictures, or video (which can be joined by content) to reach your audience with Instagram ads. The energizing part? Instagram advertising works! In March 2017, more than 120 million Instagrammers visited a website, got headings, called, messaged, or direct informed to find out about a business based on an Instagram advertisement. As indicated by Instagram, 60% of people say they find new products on the platform, and 75% of Instagrammers make a move subsequent to being enlivened by a post. Like Facebook ads, tossing some cash behind a post will prompt more introduction for your brand, just as more authority over who can see your post.

THE AMOUNT DO INSTAGRAM ADS COST?

This is a dubious inquiry to reply, as costs are based on an assortment of factors, and as you may have suspected these factors are not all uncovered to us by the platform. The model is based upon CPC (cost-per-click) and CPM's (cost per impressions), and costs are resolved by Instagram's promotion auction."The cost implication of Instagram ads are influenced by numerous factors — everything from your audience to your advertisement feedback," says Andrew Tate from AdEspresso. "A lot goes into seeing how to advertise on Instagram."AdEspresso as of late dove into $100 million worth of Instagram promotion spend in 2017, and found that the normal cost per click (CPC) for Instagram ads in Q3 ranged somewhere in the range of $0.70 and $0.80. While this is a useful benchmark it will obviously shift contingent on the sale, audience, rivalry, time of day, day of week, and so forth.

Learning the intricate details of another advertising platform may appear to be overpowering from the outset. The uplifting news here is that in case you're advertising on Facebook, there isn't a lot to learn. Actually, Instagram ads can be configured directly through Facebook Ad Manager. In case you're not advertising on Facebook, don't fuss. We'll walk you through the procedure beneath, and there is likewise the choice to make some straightforward ads legitimately inside the Instagram app. Advertisers who are further developed or running a generally huge ad set can likewise decided to configure their ads through Power Editor or Facebook's Marketing API. Instagram Partners is additionally accessible for businesses who need to purchase and deal with numerous ads, deal with an enormous network, and convey content at scale.

While configuring Instagram ads isn't excessively perplexing, there are many strides to know about. Beginning with:

1. Navigate to Facebook's Ad Manager

To navigate to ad manager inside Facebook, accepting that you're signed in to the appropriate Facebook account. Note: There is no particular Ad Manager for Instagram; Instagram ads are overseen through the Facebook Ads UI.

2. Set Your Marketing Objective

Presently for the fun part, choosing your crusade objective. Fortunately, the goals are named in a clear as crystal way. Need more traffic? Select the traffic objective. Hoping to expand brand awareness? Pick the brand awareness objective. You get the essence.

One thing to know about is that Instagram ads just work with the accompanying goals:

- Brand awareness
- App installs
- Traffic (for click through to your website or to the app store for your app)
- Reach
- Engagement (for post engagement as it were)
- Video views
- Conversions (for conversions on your app or website)

While these objectives are natural, some join a couple of additional arrangement steps, which I'll go through here.

Brand awareness: Take an extra-long lunch. No additional means here! This is the most standard objective that will attempt to show your ads to progressively potential people prone to be interested. How does Instagram decide this? It's a mystery, yet this objective will probably uncover some new and important people to your brand.

Reach: If reach is what you're searching for (as in expanding what number of people see your ads) at that point you'll simply should make certain to choose your Instagram account while making the ad itself. It's likewise significant that in case you're hoping to run an Instagram Story ad "reach" is as of now the main target you can picked. The cool thing about this objective is that you can exploit Facebook's part trying feature, which enables you to part test two ads to see which one yields more installs.

NOTE: Split testing is additionally accessible for Traffic, App Installs, Video Views, Lead Generation, and Conversion goals.

Traffic: If you're hoping to send more people to your website or app store to download your app, this is the appropriate objective for you. The main additional means you'll have to take is choosing between those two choices, at that point enter the URL of decision, and let the traffic jam in!

Engagement: Who doesn't need more likes, offers, and by and large engagement? In the event that your objective is engagement, one thing to note is that you right now can just pay to play for "post engagement" on Instagram. Facebook will enable you to pay for "page engagement" and "occasion reactions," however this isn't at present accessible to Instagram.

App Installs: If your main goal is app installs, you've gone to the correct spot. To configure this you'll have to choose your app from the app store during set-up.

Video Views: Videos are frequently a venture of time and cash, so not advancing your video on Instagram would resemble purchasing a boarding pass to Hawaii, and leaving it in your work area. Fortunately, this goal is extremely direct, and doesn't require additional setup steps.

Lead Generation: Who doesn't need more leads? In the event that that is your main goal this objective is for you. Simply note that lead age ads don't provide the entirety of the equivalent pre-filled fields as Facebook. Instagram at present just supports email, full name, telephone number, and sexual orientation. These ads likewise have all the more an obstruction than Facebook lead age ads, since when leads click to open the ad they'll have to click through to fill out their information. On Facebook, leads can fill out their information without all the additional clicking. The other set-up piece is that you'll have to create a lead form while making your ad.

Conversions: Last, however absolutely not least, we have conversions. This goal enables you to drive your leads to make a move and convert on your website or inside your app. The additional set-up here expects you to configure either a Facebook pixel or app occasion based on the website or app you're hoping to promote; this will enable you to follow conversions.

3. Configure Your Target Audience

Since you've chosen your objective, you have to target the appropriate audience to get your ads before the correct people. This is the genuine magnificence of Instagram ads since you'll be utilizing Facebook's profundity of statistic information to reach the perfect people. On the off chance that you've done this for Facebook ads before you likely already have a few audiences assembled, and are very acquainted with the process. In case you're new to this process here's a summary of your targeting options, which you can layer to get an unequivocally targeted audience. (For instance in the event that you need to target ladies, in New York, between the ages of 19 and 65, who are interested in yoga and wellbeing nourishment, you can do only that!)

Location: Whether you need to target a nation, area, state, city, postal district, avoid or include certain spots, location targeting will enable you to do the entirety of this and then some.

Age: Allows you to target ranges from age 13 to 65+

Sex: Choose between all, men, or ladies

Dialects: Facebook suggests leaving this clear except if the language you're targeting isn't regular to the location your targeting.

Demographics: Under "Definite Targeting" you'll find demographics, which has a few sub-classifications with significantly more sub-classes under those. For instance, you can target "demographics" > "Home" > "Home Ownership" > "Leaseholders."

Interests: Interests is likewise under "Itemized Targeting" with various sub-classifications to dive into. For instance, in case you're searching for people interested in refined refreshments, sci-fi motion pictures, and flying, those options are accessible for you!

Behaviors: And one more "Point by point Targeting" choice with different sub-classifications to investigate. Regardless of whether it be buying behaviors, work jobs, commemorations, or different behaviors the options appear to be perpetual.

Associations: Here you'll have the option to target people associated with your page, app, or occasion.

Custom Audience: Custom audiences let you upload your very own rundown of contacts enabling you to target leads already in your pipeline or customers who you're looking to upsell.

Lookalike Audience: If your custom audience is tapped to their potential, create a lookalike audience. This will permit Instagram to find people who have comparative characteristics to your different audiences.

When you've configured your audience, Facebook will likewise provide you with a manual for how explicit or broad your audience.

This is a significant tool to pay attention to, in light of the fact that you need to find some kind of harmony of your audience not being excessively tremendous (since it's presumable not targeted enough), yet additionally not being excessively explicit (in the red zone), since there may not be numerous people (assuming any) to reach with such a significant number of layered targets.

App Installs: If your main goal is app installs, you've gone to the right spot. To configure this you'll need to choose your app from the app store during set-up.

Video Views: Videos are every now and again an endeavor of time and money, so not advancing your video on Instagram would take after buying a ticket to Hawaii, and leaving it in your work zone.

Luckily, this goal is incredibly direct, and doesn't require additional setup steps.

Lead Generation: Who doesn't require more leads? In the event that that is your main goal this objective is for you. Just note that lead age ads don't provide the entirety of the comparable pre-filled fields as Facebook. Instagram at present just supports email, full name, phone number, and sexual direction. These ads in like manner have all the more a deterrent than Facebook lead age ads, since when leads click to open the ad they'll need to click through to fill out their information. On Facebook, leads can fill out their information without all the additional clicking. The other set-up piece is that you'll need to create a lead form while making your ad.

Conversions: Last, anyway in no way, shape or form least, we have conversions. This goal enables you to drive your leads to make a move and convert on your website or inside your app. The additional set-up here anticipates that you should configure either a Facebook pixel or app event based on the website or app you're planning to promote; this will enable you to follow conversions.

4. Configure Your Target Audience

Since you've picked your objective, you need to target the appropriate audience to get your ads before the right people. This is the authentic heavenliness of Instagram ads since you'll be using Facebook's significance of measurement information to reach the ideal people. In case you've done this for Facebook ads before you likely already have a couple of audiences amassed, and are exceptionally familiar with the process. On the off chance that you're new to this process here's a rundown of your targeting options, which you can layer to get an unequivocally targeted audience. (For instance in the event that you have to target ladies, in New York, between the ages of 19 and 65, who are interested in yoga and prosperity sustenance, you can do just that!)

Location: Whether you have to target a country, territory, state, city, postal region, maintain a strategic distance from or include certain spots, location targeting will enable you to do the entirety of this to say the very least.

Age: Allows you to target ranges from age 13 to 65+

Sex: Choose between all, men, or ladies

Vernaculars: Facebook proposes leaving this reasonable aside from if the language you're targeting isn't ordinary to the location your targeting.

Demographics: Under "Positive Targeting" you'll find demographics, which has a couple of sub-orders with fundamentally more sub-classes under those. For instance, you can target "demographics" > "Home" > "Home Ownership" > "Leaseholders."

Interests: Interests is in like manner under "Ordered Targeting" with different sub-characterizations to jump into. For instance, in the event that you're searching for people interested in refined refreshments, science fiction films, and flying, those options are open for you!

Behaviors: And one more "Point by point Targeting" decision with various sub-characterizations to research. Notwithstanding whether it be purchasing behaviors, work employments, celebrations, or various behaviors the options appear to be interminable.

Relationship: Here you'll have the choice to target people related with your page, app, or event.

Custom Audience: Custom audiences let you upload your own one of a kind overview of contacts empowering you to target leads already in your pipeline or customers who you're looking to upsell.

Lookalike Audience: If your custom audience is tapped to their potential, create a lookalike audience. This will allow Instagram to find people who have similar qualities to your various audiences.

At the point when you've configured your audience, Facebook will moreover provide you with a manual for how unequivocal or broad your audience.

This is a critical tool to pay attention to, considering the way that you have to find some sort of agreement of your audience not being too much huge (since it's apparent not targeted enough), yet additionally not being too much unequivocal (in the red zone), since there may not be various people (expecting any) to reach with such countless layered targets.

INSTAGRAM AD FORMATS

On the off chance that you are a bad decision, aker, you might need to prepare yourself. Instagram has six ad formats to choose from. (This is path less than Facebook!) Two of those are for Instagram stories, which appear at the highest point of the feed in a way like Snapchats. The other four are formats designed for the Instagram feed, which are all the more usually utilized by advertisers.

1. IMAGE FEED ADS

This is your most standard ad format, and likely the one you see regularly scrolling through your own feed. These ads are single images that will appear as a local encounter as your target lead is scrolling through their feed. The dazzling thing about these ads is that they don't feel like ads, particularly when done well. Here are some additional subtleties to know about:

Technical Requirements
- File type: jpg or png
- Maximum record size: 30MB
- Minimum Image Width: 600 pixels
- Image Ratio: 4:5 minimum, 16:9 most extreme
- Text length: 2,200 most extreme (*although Instagram prescribes remaining beneath 90 for ideal conveyance)
- Hashtag Number: 30 most extreme (*you can add additional in the remarks)

Supported Objectives
- Reach
- Traffic
- Conversions
- App Installs
- Lead Generation
- Brand Awareness
- Post Engagement
- Product Catalog Sales
- Store Visits

Supported Call-to-Action
- Buttons
- Apply Now
- Book Now

- Call Now
- Contact Us
- Get Directions
- Learn More
- Get Showtimes
- Download

2. *IMAGE STORY ADS*

Same idea as above, however these are for Instagram stories! Subtleties underneath:

Technical Requirements
- Image Ratio: 9:16 prescribed
- Minimum Image Width: 600 pixels

Supported Objectives
- Reach
- Traffic
- Conversions
- App Installs
- Lead Generation

Supported Call-to-Action
- Buttons
- Apply Now
- Book Now
- Contact Us
- Download

3. VIDEO FEED ADS

Breath life into your ad with a video! If you've placed the time in to make a quality video, at that point you ought to totally be advancing it through your Instagram feed. While most video records are supported by Instagram, they prescribe utilizing H.264 pressure, square pixels, fixed edge rate, dynamic output, and stereo AAC sound pressure at 128kbps+ (PRO TIP: if your video isn't meeting these prerequisite you can generally run it through the video transcoder, Handbrake, to make these adjustments).

Technical Requirements

- Video Resolution: 1080 x 1080 pixels (at any rate)
- Maximum file size: 4GB
- Video Ratio: 4:5 minimum,16:9 maximum
- Video Duration: 60 seconds maximum
- Video Captions: discretionary
- Image Ratio: 4:5 minimum, 16:9 maximum
- Text length: 125 characters maximum suggested
- Hashtag Number: 30 maximum (*you can add additional in the remarks)

Supported Objectives
- Reach
- Traffic
- Conversions
- Lead Generation
- Brand Awareness
- Post Engagement
- Store Visits

Supported Call-to-Action
- Buttons
- Apply Now
- Book Now
- Call Now
- Contact Us
- Download

4. VIDEO STORY ADS

This is another great spot to run video ads, since stories are the place clients regularly hope to see videos, so the "selling" part of advertising doesn't feel as constrained. The suggested video specs for uploading are equivalent to recorded above, and here are some additional subtleties to remember!

Technical Requirements
- Video Resolution: 1080 x 1920 pixels (in any event)
- Maximum file size: 4GB

- Video Ratio: 9:16 maximum
- Video Duration: 15 seconds maximum
- Video Captions: not accessible

Supported Objectives
- Reach
- Traffic
- Conversions
- Lead Generation
- App Installs

Supported Call-to-Action
- Buttons
- Apply Now
- Book Now
- Call Now
- Contact Us
- Download

5. *Carousel Feed Ads*

Next we have carousel feed ads. How fun are these! This format enables you to show a progression of scrollable images as opposed to only one single image. This ad type great for extremely visual brands, similar to those in the nourishment business, furniture sellers, clothing options, get-away destinations, vehicle vendors, and so on. Yet, they're not just for "hot" businesses; they can likewise work to refine your brand or show off your way of life by showing the people behind your product or money related company. The carousel format enables you to choose from up to 10 images inside a solitary ad, each with its own link. Video is likewise a possibility for these ads.

Technical Requirements

File type: jpg or png

Maximum file size: 30MB

Minimum Image Width: 600 pixels

Image Ratio: 4:5 minimum, 16:9 maximum

Text length: 2,200 maximum (*although Instagram recommends staying below 90 for optimal delivery)

Video Duration: 60 seconds maximum

Hashtag Number: 30 maximum (*you can add additional in the comments)

Supported Objectives

Reach

Traffic

Conversions

Brand Awareness

Lead Generation

Product Catalog Sales

Supported Call-to-Action

Buttons

Apply Now

Book Now
Contact Us
Call Now
Download

6. CANVAS STORY ADS

And last, but definitely not least, we have the newest addition to the ad format family, Canvas ads. There ads are truly immersive, allowing advertising to create a 360 VR experience within their story. They're only supported via mobile devices, and extremely customizable for the advertiser, but you will need some technical chops. These ads work with image, video, and carousel. Check out this guide to learn more about Canvas ads.

Technical Requirements
Minimum Image Width: 400 pixels
Minimum Image Height: 150 pixels

Supported Objectives
Reach
Brand Awareness
Traffic
Conversions
Lead Generation
Post Engagement
Video Views

Store Visits

Supported Call-to-Action
Buttons
Apply Now
Book Now
Contact Us

5. INSTAGRAM ADVERTISING BEST PRACTICES

Since you have the fundamental standards of Instagram advertising down, the time has come to get the most elevated ROI conceivable by following these prescribed procedures to create great Instagram ads.

1. Instill Each Ad with Personality

Regardless of whether it be an amusing goof, a passionate video, or only a captivating image showing off your way of life, on the off chance that your Instagram post doesn't feel acculturated, at that point you won't reach your engagement potential. People use Instagram to be engaged, diverted, or flabbergasted. Regardless of whether it's while you're on the train to work or when you are loosening up in the wake of a monotonous day of work, nobody is hoping to bounce on Instagram to see an exhausting corporate advertisement. This is the reason appealing to feelings is consistently the best approach. Look at this fun post from Shape Magazine as an ideal model.

2. Make Sure Your Ad Is Contextually Relevant

What works with one social media platform won't really work with another. For instance, your business likely wouldn't promote a similar content through LinkedIn as they would through Twitter, as the audience is typically in an alternate perspective. The equivalent goes for Instagram. Put yourself in your target purchaser's shoes and know about where they are. On Instagram, do you think your lead is probably going to download and read your 40 page digital book? Most likely not. Guarantee your ads don't feel excessively sales-driven in light of the fact that this isn't typically what Instagram is utilized for.

3. Use Hashtags...

Be that as it may, don't simply hashtag #food or #love. Get progressively inventive, and do some client research to see which hashtags are bound to be searched for by your audience. Likewise, don't try too hard with hashtags. This can make your post look somewhat messy and desperate. The ideal number? TrackMaven broke down 65,000 posts and found that 9 hashtags is the ideal number for most elevated post engagement. They likewise found that longer hashtags regularly perform better.

4. Run a Contest

Advancing a contest or giveaway is by a wide margin one of the best approaches to reach your goals quicker with Instagram advertising. Why? Since people love competition and free stuff! What better approach to get your audience amped up for your brand?

5. Post at Optimal Hours

If you realize your audience well, this shouldn't be too difficult to even consider determining, yet experimentation can likewise work here. Consider your vertical. In case you're an online retailer, when do people commonly search for clothing on the web? Or then again in case you're a vehicle vendor, what days of the week do you see the most noteworthy spike in website traffic? Posing these inquiries is a decent spot to begin. Right away, put forward and advertise on Instagram! This is one platform you ought not disregard, and this guide ought to give you enough assets to become insta-famous.

What are these stats?

• The number of clicks: this refers to the number of clicks your Ad has received from users

• The Post likes: this refers to the number of likes your Ad has achieved

• The Cost per click: this refers to the total cost of each click on your Ad

• The Cost per view: this refers to the total cost per impression of your Ad

• Click through rates: this refers to the percentage of clicks through to your landing page the Ad has achieved in relation to the number of impressions

• Cost per lead: this refers to the overall cost of gaining a lead via your Ad

• Lead to customer conversion: this refers to the number of leads who become your customers via your Instagram Ad

The number of clicks and post likes you receive on your Ad will give you an idea of the efficiency of the image you have chosen: the more clicks, the better the image.

The cost per click (CPC), the cost per view and the cost per lead are the figures that represent how much the advertising process is costing you at each step: the most important figure being the cost per lead, as this tells you exactly how much each new lead acquired via your campaign has cost your company. Another important figure is the lead to customer conversion, which is the number of leads who go on to become customers as a direct result of this Ad.

The click through rate (CTR) is also an important figure, as it will tell you the percentage of users who not only saw your Ad, but who actually followed your call to action straight through to your website or landing page. This number will give you an idea of how effective your image and text choices for your Ad are at getting attention and deserving clicks.

Influencer Marketing Research Tools

If you decided not to use a platform or an agency for your influencer marketing then you will have to build up relationships with influencers yourself. To do this, you first need to know the influencers that rule your niche. If you are an active online participant in your niche you may already possess a good idea who are the best influencers. In other cases, you will have to carry out considerable research first. Luckily there are a variety of influencer marketing tools to help you in your quest.

In the event that you are searching for an agency to run your campaign - feel free to utilize our agency coordinating structure underneath and you will be coordinated with the most appropriate agency for your needs. You should think about where you would like to find your potential influencers. Many operate via web-based networking media, so a portion of these tools center around finding the notable people in the internet based life channels. You should initially think about where your intended interest group invests its energy. If you target more seasoned people, for instance, you will frequently search for influencers in Facebook groups discussing your niche. In the event that your objective market is youngsters, at that point you may concentrate more on Snapchat, Youtube or Instagram. Numerous influencers have picked up their popularity from blogs they compose. We have a couple of tools here that assist you with finding the persuasive bloggers in your niche.

There is a lot of proof that influencer marketing can be an exceptionally effective strategy for spreading a brand's message. At the point when the Influencer Marketing Hub attempted an overview on the condition of influencer marketing a year ago, we found that the normal earned media esteem per $1 spent on influencer marketing was a profoundly respectable $7.65.We have likewise observed a fast ascent in the utilization of Instagram in the course of the most recent couple of years, to the point where it would now be able to guarantee more than 800 million month to month dynamic clients. Instagram Stories has likewise observed quick growth and is currently has a greater number of clients than Snapchat.

It makes sense for most brands to work with influencers on Instagram. In any case, on the off chance that you will do that you need first to find influencers who are happy to work with you. On the off chance that you depend on building connections naturally, suitable influencers can be trying to find, and it will be a time-devouring procedure to create and support connections. That is the place the influencer platforms can give a helpful assistance. Influencer platforms can be a definitive tool to disentangle your influencer marketing. Various platforms have practical experience in the services they offer, however the most well-known ones are:

Influencer discovery

Relationship management

Campaign management

Influencer marketplace

Third party analytics

Influencer content amplification

Every one of the platforms centers around giving influencer services to particular interpersonal organizations. With Instagram quickly turning into the network of decision for influencers, it is nothing unexpected that by far most of influencer platforms include Instagram in their contributions. Here are the leading influencer platforms for Instagram that can assist you with your influencer search and make your influencer marketing a smoother, progressively streamlined procedure.

1. AspireIQ (formerly known as Revfluence)

AspireIQ (some time ago Revfluence) has the profiles of more than 500,000 influencers in its discovery motor. Its calculation creeps the web searching through social accounts to find people who meet its influencer criteria. In any case, if an influencer needs to effectively participate in campaigns through the AspireIQ platform, they first need to pick into the framework. AspireIQ gives various approaches to brands to find influencers. You can search utilizing applicable watchwords, points, or hashtags, and afterward filter accounts by whatever strategy you need. You can utilize the "Quickmatch" feature, which recommends influencers based on your inclinations. Another way you can find influencers is to utilize AspireIQ's Watchlist feature, which will disclose to you which influencers have referenced you or your rivals. You can even search by picture – searching for influencers who have shared content like a particular picture. AspireIQ covers significantly more than just influencer discovery, be that as it may. It has powerful tools that can help brands with:

- Campaign creation
- Campaign lifecycle management
- Digital term sheets
- Product following
- Content cooperation
- Trackable sales links
- Creator execution spreadsheet

- Campaign analytics
- Payments

2. Neoreach

Neoreach has manufactured a calculation that digs the social web for information. Their database contains the social subtleties of more than 3 million influencers. The company targets huge organizations and undertakings.

You start your influencer search with keywords, and afterward refine the outcomes utilizing a range of factors, including:

- Conversation point
- Social channel
- Social measurements
- Audience psychographics and demographics.

It gives you an abundance of data, and you can sort influencers into groups or campaigns. Neoreach additionally utilizes AI to prescribe suitable influencers for your needs. The more you use Neoreach, the more accurate their proposals will be. When you have discovered influencers, you can utilize Neoreach's campaign management tools to help your influencer marketing run all the more easily. It includes an incorporated interchanges center point, to keep the whole influencer relationship process together. Campaign reports are exceptionally nitty gritty, letting you know for all intents and purposes anything there is to think about campaign execution. Neoreach has built up their own proportion of ROI – Influencer Media Value (IMV). You just need to connect your advertising spend to the model, and Neoreach will give you an accurate gauge of IMV for your future influencer campaigns.

Services Offered: Influencer Discovery, Campaign Management

3. Upfluence

Upfluence has made significant changes to its offerings over the last year. It has narrowed the range of services it offers, concentrating on what it believes are its strengths. The heart of Upfluence is its massive database containing nearly 1 million influencers. It indexes and updates social profiles in real time, analyzing every item of content for reach and engagement. Brands can search Upfluence to find influencers using any combination of relevant keywords. They can then drill down and refine their selection of influencers. You can even weight your keywords, placing more emphasis on some than others. You can filter by audience data, including psychographic attributes like cultural interests and brand affinities. Upfluence allows you to make lists of potential influencers meeting various criteria, which you can export into CSV files. You can manage your influencer within Upfluence, including keeping a central repository for all email correspondence. The lifecycle management function keeps track of your progress with each influencer.

Services Offered: Influencer Discovery, Campaign Management

4. Tagger Media

Tagger Media is a pick in influencer marketplace with more than 1 million influencers in its database. It tracks 8 billion social discussions that make more than 28 million information focuses. You can search for influencers utilizing 50 filters to assist you with refining the outcomes. Tagger Media offers substantially more than only an influencer search motor, be that as it may. It is a full influencer marketplace, designed to enable huge businesses to find and work with its monstrous database of influencers. It is an across the board platform that enables brands to:

• Perform point by point searches on the database of clients

• Discover influencers to work with

• Create campaigns, making them just accessible to welcomed influencers or then again to anyone

• Manage chose influencers and their content entries

• Analyze post and influencer execution

• Determine important ROI

Tagger Media puts a critical accentuation on psychographics. It investigations what people are discussing, their inclinations and their affinities. This enables clients to comprehend what content will drive engagement. It likewise features an exceptionally vigorous management dashboard, making it easy for firms to arrange their influencer marketing endeavors.

Services Offered: Influencer Discovery, Campaign Management, Influencer Marketplace, Third Party Analytics.

5. Julius

Julius has grown from being exclusively an influencer discovery motor into a fully-fledged self-administration marketing suite. Despite everything it features an incredible influencer search motor, in any case, with a variety of information identifying with its 120,000 fully checked influencers. You can search for influencers utilizing 50 unique criteria to limit your search. These spread both statistic and psychographic factors. Julius enables you to add any influencers you presently work with who aren't already in their framework. The Julius staff vet these people and add their applicable information to the database. Julius gives you various approaches to search for suitable influencers. It features a particularly easy-to-utilize interface. You can search by criteria identifying with potential

51

influencers, your intended interest group, or social reach and engagement. You can rapidly make records based on the criteria you are utilizing. Julius likewise features a strong arrangement of campaign management tools, again designed In a reasonable, easy-to-utilize style. You can without much of a stretch find out anything you need to think about your campaign with only a couple of catch clicks. The strong clean approach extends to announcing too. It gives clear easy-to-read perceptions of your influencers' presentation on each campaign.

Services Offered: Influencer Discovery, Campaign Management, Third Party Analytics.

6. HYPR

HYPR has built a massive database of more than 10 million influencers and makes a point of collecting as much demographic data about their followers as possible. They consider their search engine to be "talent agnostic," i.e., they don't limit their results to showing just a list of influencers who have agreed to work with them. The search engine is the heart of HYPR. It is very much the Google of influencers. It uses a simple, but highly responsive interface, leading to a quick return of search results. Although you could search for an influencer you know by name, the bulk of your searches will be by audience. HYPR believes the key to successful influencer marketing is matching up influencer with target audiences. You can search by audience interest and by a range of demographic factors, such as gender, ethnicity, and age group. You can then refine your searches further, by looking at factors such as influencer location and follower counts. Once you have made your list, HYPR will present you with influencers who meet your criteria. Each influencer shows up on a little card, showing their photo and a summary of relevant details. If you believe somebody looks suitable, you can click on their card to see more information about their audience and social reach.

Services Offered: Influencer Discovery

7. MAVRCK

As its name indicates, Mavrck aims to take a different approach to influencer marketing. Most platforms will provide you with a list of people who are already popular on social media but don't necessarily know your product. Mavrck's approach is to take your existing customers and encourage them to promote your product online. Mavrck takes your existing customer list and determines who has the most influence online. You begin by setting up a white-labeled standalone website, or you add a plugin to your existing website. Customers log into your site using their Facebook profile. Mavrck finds all the public social data connected to each customer. It can then use its algorithm to determine each customer's social influence.

If Mavrck finds a customer to be sufficiently influential it automatically activates a suitable campaign for him or her. Mavrck has a list of 20 'digital activities' different customer influencers can do, depending on their level of influence. Your customers receive rewards for completing each 'digital activity' you offer them. You can use all of the content created by your micro-influencer customers to attract new customers – who may, in turn, become micro-influencers on behalf of your brand. Mavrck provides you with a detailed dashboard showing a considerable amount of information about your campaigns.

Services Offered: Influencer Discovery, Relationship Management, Campaign Management, Influencer Marketplace, Third Party Analytics.

8. Influencer

Influencer tags itself as being "run by creators, for creators." Indeed its Chief Marketing Officer (CMO) is Caspar Lee, who is renowned as a YouTube star. It's founder, Ben Jeffries, was only 18 when he started the business. It is very much a product of Generation Z. With Influencer being run by influencers, it should be easy to distinguish genuine influencers. It is fussier about who it accepts onto their books. They are only interested in people with many real followers and a high level of engagement. This means that Influencer has established a reputation as only working with talent who can easily communicate with their followers. This means that customers will only find about 1,000 influencers on their database – but they are all highly influential onliners. Because Influencer has a more hands-on process than their more automated competitors, it does limit itself geographically. It is headquartered in the UK and currently focuses on influencers who have audiences based in Europe. Although Influencer is a platform, it offers many of the features of a boutique agency. It includes all the expected management tools to assist with your campaigns. Services Offered: Influencer Marketplace.

9. Traackr

Traackr is one of the earliest influencer marketing tools – the first Traackr product was released in 2008. The company has changed its offerings as the industry developed and now specializes in influencer relationship management, built on top of an impressive online platform with an array of influencer management tools. Although the platform focuses more on influencer relationship than influencer discovery, it does include a robust search engine. It provides numerous search and filter options to help brands find the ideal influencers for their campaigns. Traackr takes a hybrid approach to its influencer database – a combination of human involved in curation mixed with algorithms collecting data. Traackr offers you many ways you can organize your selected influencers. One of these is to sort your influencers by relationship stage. This makes it easy to segment your influencers by how close you are. Traackr allows you to customize the data you store about your influencers. It also records all communications you or members of your team have with them. Traackr incorporates a social listening tool which allows you to track your influencer content in real time. You can filter this however you want, so you are not swamped by irrelevant details. Another useful tool is Traackr's network visualization map. This shows you how influencers are connected with other people, both within and outside your network. This gives you a clear idea of who influences your influencers, and may give you further suggestions for building relationships. Traackr provides a powerful set of campaign management tools, that makes running campaigns appear simple. You can even track how much your campaigns influence conversation.

Services Offered: Relationship Management, Campaign Management

Deciding Your Price as an Influencer

Instagram influencer rates are one of online networking's best-kept secrets. Sure, there are murmurs and bits of gossip, similar to Kendall Jenner's accounted for $250,000 pull for her Fyre Festival underwriting on Instagram. In any case, what precisely are the computations that go into making influencer marketing a $6.5 billion industry? For a plethora of Instagram influencers, a sponsored post includes a lot more work than posting an orange square. (For those not aware of everything, Fyre Festival promoters made buzz by paying large scale influencers to post an orange jpeg.)Creating branded content includes time, work, ability, and creation costs. What's more, those things aren't paid for with products and freebies. And paying the correct value pays off. In any case, what is the privilege price? Read on to find the best recipe for figuring rates, the advantages of various sponsorship plans, and different elements that may influence influencer valuing.

The fundamental equation for figuring reasonable Instagram influencer rates

There are numerous elements that decide the rate an influencer charges for their work. Most estimating beginnings with this gauge recipe and goes up from that point. $100 x 10,000 followers + additional items = all out rate Typically, influencers will have a press pack portraying their rates and the sorts of partnerships accessible. Contingent upon the crusade, bundled content or exceptional rates can likewise be worked out to lessen work and costs.

What kind of influencer is directly for your objectives?

From individual fund to plant-based influencers there are micro, full scale, and power center influencers in each class. Contingent upon your Instagram marketing objectives, certain influencers might be a superior counterpart for your brand.

If your objective is brand-awaareness

For brands hoping to make far reaching buzz, full scale influencers with enormous supporter accounts might be the best wagered. Full scale influencers ordinarily have in excess of 200,000 followers, which gives them the capacity to reach a more extensive group of spectators.

IF YOUR OBJECTIVE IS CONVERSIONS

An influencer's engagement rate is one of the most dependable approaches to foresee changes on Instagram. Engagement rates can be determined by including up all engagements a post (likes, remarks, clicks, shares), isolating by adherent tally, and increasing by 100.The normal engagement rate on Instagram is 2.1 percent.

If your objective is changes, an influencer's engagement rate may matter more than supporter check. Here's the place control center influencers (25,000-200,000 followers) regularly come in. For instance, a power-center influencer with 179K followers and a high engagement rate will probably be a superior partner than a full scale influencer with a lower engagement rate. Some influencers may charge more than $100 per 10,000 followers in the event that they have a higher than normal rate of engagement.

IF YOUR GOAL IS TO GAIN A NICHE AUDIENCE

Micro influencers have 25,000 followers or less, and are all the time mainstream in area or subject explicit networks. They work in a range of

59

businesses of classes, including anything from sports and gaming, to travel and nourishment. Group of spectators sizes of niche influencers can range from micro to full scale. For instance, excellence influencer Hudda Kattan has an astounding 33 million followers. In the event that your brand falls into a niche classification, it's advantageous to delineate the micro influencers in your industry's social network. A decent brand fit is imperative to influencers, and will prompt an increasingly authentic and effective battle. Niche influencers may charge more than the essential rate for the mastery they bring to their particular group of spectators.

Types of Instagram posts and partnerships

There are various approaches to collaborate with influencers on Instagram. Here we separate the principle things and arrangements Instagram influencers charge for. We additionally feature every one of their unique benefits.

Instagram photo

A standard sponsored Instagram post ordinarily includes a photo and caption. Sometimes the product is included in the picture. In different cases, similar to when an assistance is being promoted, the caption is increasingly significant.

Benefits of an Instagram photo:

• It's anything but difficult to foresee and follow post execution.

• Partnership disclaimers can be added obviously. Product and brand labeling can be added.

• Tagging can be fortified in the caption too.

• Super short links can be added to the caption.

• Allows for authentic narrating.

• Can be additionally promoted in an Instagram story.

Instagram slideshow

The key distinction between an Instagram post and slideshow is that a slideshow permits an influencer to build to a greater degree a story, or showcase the sponsorship in various ways. Nonetheless, added content will include added costs–particularly if various shoots are required.

Benefits of an Instagram slideshow:

• Offers numerous ways for a group of people to connect with content.

• Features various products or use-cases for your brand.

• Creates more space for an influencer to include their authentic take.

- Allows for increasingly unpredictable or nuanced narrating.

Instagram video

Video's star continues to rise on social, and Instagram is no different, tracking an 80 % year-over-year increment. Most content creators appreciate that a video involves greater production costs than a photo, but the added investment can often translate into more than just added engagement.

Benefits of Instagram video:

Gives the influencer a voice, literally.

This often shows the influencer's audience a new side person they follow.

Allows for compelling storytelling.

Builds bundling potential. Consider working teasers or behind-the-scenes posts or Instagram Stories into a video shoot.

Instagram giveaway or contest

Instagram contests are a great method to grow brand awareness and followers. Commonly a contest involves approaching a client to accomplish something for a chance to win a prize, regardless of whether it's labeling a friend, preferring your account, or sharing a post.

Benefits of an Instagram contest:

- Reaches a wider extensive group of spectators with a little cost-per-engagement.
- Earns group of audience data, particularly if your contest involves a brief like "remark with your fantasy destination and label a friend."
- Puts your product or administration up front.

Instagram Story

An Instagram story is basically a photo or video that evaporates following 24 hours. Production quality can range from without any preparation cell phone film to cleaned uploaded content, and costs will differ in like manner

Benefits of an Instagram Story

Regularly looks increasingly easygoing and authentic.

Permits the influencer to include character through GIFs, markups, and sticks.

Noticeable labeling can be added all the more effectively.

Influencers can be valuable about their feed's stylish, yet will in general be progressively adaptable with Story content.

One disadvantage about Instagram Stories is that they're more enthusiastically to follow.

Instagram's API offers restricted retrievable information. That and they vanish except if featured (you can pay extra to have your content included in an influencers Story Highlights).

Instagram Story with swipe up

The swipe up feature on Instagram is a consistent method to acquire in-application conversions. Also, since links are difficult to find in Instagram's environment, story swipe ups have added esteem. Contingent upon the influencer, swipe ups can cost more.

Benefits of an Instagram Story with swipe up:

• Provides a cost-viable approach to acquire changes and quality leads.

• Allows your brand to include setting with a particular or custom greeting page.

• Offers a dependable way to check group of spectators enthusiasm for your brand.

• Brings customers a bit nearer to making a buy.

In case you're working with a micro-influencer that has less than 10,000 followers or isn't confirmed, they might not approach this feature.

Instagram Story with poll

Adding a poll to an Instagram Story is a low-cost way to learn more about an influencer's followers (and your prospective customers).

Benefits of an Instagram Story with a poll:
Captures immediate feedback from the influencer's audience in a fun way.
Posting poll results is another low-cost way to increase exposure by another 24 hours.

Brand takeover
A brand takeover usually involves hosting the influencer's content on your brand's feed for an agreed upon length of time. A takeover agreement may involve asks for the influencer to promote it a certain number of times from their account–in posts and/or Stories.

Benefits of a brand takeover:
Brings the influencer's followers to your account.
Helps to increase brand awareness.
Promotes influencer's content and perspective, which often comes across as more authentic.
Opens the door for bundle or special rate agreements. Influencers should always be paid, but if your brand can offer special tours or access, that can be factored in as well.

Story Highlights
Having an influencer highlight branded stories extends the expiry date of that content. This will also put your brand in prime real estate on their account's profile. However, high visibility like this will come at a higher cost.

Benefits of Story Highlights

Maximum exposure. On an Instagram profile, highlights are positioned above the feed, meaning brand placement here is a step above photos or videos.

Stories won't be highlighted forever, but they live longer than 24 hours and increase the odds that they'll reach more viewers.

Increases conversions. If the highlighted story includes a swipe-up, it's likely you'll earn more visits and leads, for a longer time.

Link in Bio

The only place where links are active on Instagram is in a person's account bio. If you're planning to sponsor an influencer post, it may be worthwhile to invest more by asking them to promote a link from their bio.

Benefits of Link in Bio:

Prime visibility. Someone may miss a post or story, but if they visit an influencer's profile they'll see your link. Consider asking the influencer to include a call-to-action in their bio as well.

Increases traffic. If your brand is angling to drive visitors to a certain webpage, this is one of the best ways to do it on

Instagram.IGTV

IGTV is the longer form video vertical on Instagram. It has pride of place on the platform, appearing at the top of the feed, in the explore tab, and next to highlights on a user's feed. Because IGTV typically involves higher production and has high visibility, it will involve higher costs.

Benefits of IGTV:

Boosts visibility of content in the app.

If the influencer is verified and has enough followers, they can post vertical videos up to 60 minutes in length, allowing for long-form storytelling.

IGTV videos can include clickable links.

Other factors that affect Instagram influencer pricing

Brands in search of quality partnerships should budget for these cost factors when marketing with influencers.

Usage rights

If you want to maintain ownership of the content you create with an influencer, so that you can use it on other platforms or down the line, this will likely impact the influencer's rate.

Production fees

Various production related costs such as how long it takes to produce the content (labor), props, clothing, hair and makeup, photography, editing, and travel, should be factored into influencer rates.

Agency fees

Many influencers are represented by managers or agencies such as Crowdtap, Niche, Tapinfluencer, or Maker Studios. These companies will typically charge handling fees.

Campaign length

The length of the campaign will have a direct affect on influencer pricing based on the added labour, content, and exclusivity requirements attached to it.

Timing

Depending on how much time a brand gives an influencer to create content, a rush fee may be applied.

Exclusivity

Most contracts include an exclusivity clause, in which the influencer agrees not to work with competitors for a determined length of time. Since this could cost influencers prospective deals, it will affect the cost.

Brand fit

If an influencer feels that a company lacks a level of affinity with their personal brand, they may charge for what the partnership may cost them in credibility.

Experts in the field of marketing likewise discovered that, the best method to reach out to potential buyers in this century would be through the people these buyers pursue and trust on social stages like Instagram. It's basic extremely: A lot of people trust the proposals of genuine people, other than those of sponsors. As time cruises by, innovation has made more ways for people to debilitate and square promotions. Further constraining organizations to reach out to influencers to get their products and brand before their potential buyers. Be that as it may, the issue a lot of influencers have is realizing the amount they should charge their clients. Many do not have the required data and frantically need to know whether they are under or cheating their clients.

At the point when you get enlisted to do a sponsored post, it's not quite the same as customary content creation, on the grounds that the brand is paying for you to post – which implies: introduction, eyeballs, sees, clicks (you get where we're going with this). This is the reason you should consistently be straightforward with your examination and your influence.

If you don't feel like your capacity to drive clicks is there at this time, be forthright with the brand and tell them that you might want to create a specific measure of photos for them notwithstanding posting on Instagram. Along these lines you can post a couple on your page, yet in addition send them extra photos for them to post on their account on the grounds that toward the day's end, each brand is consistently needing great Instagram photos for their feed as well. Furthermore, when you are not certain about the intensity of your influence, the key is to OVERDELIVER.

ASKING THE BRAND FOR A BUDGET

You ought to consistently begin any sponsorship discussion with asking what their budget is (obviously you ought to have a main concern as a primary concern since anything lower than that number is simply not justified, despite any potential benefits to you).By approaching the brand for their budget first, you can (a) think of a proposition dependent on their needs, (b) save yourself time from making a recommendation that isn't in their value run and the in particular (c) save yourself from passing up additional cold hard cash... imagine a scenario where they are eager to pay WAY more than what you were anticipating proposing. In any case, imagine a scenario where they state there is no budget and they need you to do the post for exchange. Sadly, free swag doesn't pay the bills – yet a little doesn't hurt, correct? Obviously there are consistently special cases if it's an item or experience you need in your life! We've worked with celebrity influencers (2+ million followers) who have gone on trips for nothing due to every one of the advantages that join them.

So at last, every partnership or sponsorship descends how might this benefit YOU! What's more, in case you're consulting with a travel industry board or lodging that has offered to pay for the entirety of your movement costs, and you have another brand ready to pay for a sponsorship, at that point you'll need to tell them that you'll be bringing along a sponsor to pay for ability expenses. To make sure you know, 9 times out of 10, the travel industry loads up will cover flights, housing, transport, nourishment, drink and exercises, yet perhaps nothing else outside of that. That is the reason you'll need to reach out to another brand (that lines up with the destination), to check whether they are keen on having their products shot in the fascinating destination, to assist you with getting paid.

Be that as it may, remember to be proficient and make sure the sponsor willing to pony up money lines up with the destination you are made a beeline for in light of the fact that else it might cause issues. For instance, asking a caffeinated drink company to sponsor an outing to Costa Rica, would not make sense with Costa Rica's homestead to table ethos. We're enthusiastic about press trip manners since we know how significant cultivating connections are and how these trips can really find you more occupations not far off. Finally, we must pressure this as much as possible – don't simply accept the position due to the cash. Continuously make sure every partnership and sponsorship you acknowledge lines up with your brand esteems and objectives... essentially, don't be shallow.

INSTAGRAM PRICE PER POST – THE BASICS

Before we delve into the nitty gritty on pricing, we need to define "post" because it will determine how you price yourself.

Instagram post – photo: posting a permanent post on your Instagram account using specific hashtags, tags, geotags etc.

Instagram post – video: posting a permanent video on your Instagram account using specific hashtags, tags, geotags and even an audio mention.

Instagram story: promoting on a story and using a specific hashtag and tag and even an audio mention.

And if you work in an Instagram story, you'll have the option to provide it on your Instagram "highlights" as an additional value added feature. According to Adweek, the average price per sponsored post is about $300, with influencers that have 100,000 followers earning closer to $800 a post. While everyone wants a magic formula, we know there is no one-size-fits-all approach...this is the wild west, after all! That's why we're covering three different ways you can establish your "insta rate." So for all those wondering "how much is my instagram post worth," below are three different ways to come up with your price.

OPTION 1: CHARGE AN HOURLY RATE

Charging by an hourly rate can be a great option for beginners who don't have a large following or engagement but still feel like you could produce quality content. This is a good bet for micro-influencers (less than 10,000 organic, authentic followers).Opting for an hourly rate is also great for a freelancer with a special skillset (i.e. graphic design, copywriter, photographer etc). You can also offer different hourly rates depending on what exactly you will be doing for the brand. In some cases, people like to charge more for their time if it involves a technical skill. For example, if you're reviewing a product versus creating a video or taking product photos- the latter two involve way more effort which means you should be compensated for your time. If you're using a drone, doing any special effects or using some technical editing skills, you may want to charge more for that time as well.

So what's the formula?

Hourly rate (* hours needed to produce) + any extra costs

Optional: Hourly rate (* hours needed to produce) + Speciality Hourly Rate (* hours needed to produce) + any extra costs

Any additional expenses could include the accompanying – props, colleague work, travel costs and so on. Everyones hourly rate is distinctive dependent on what they have to make a living so you have to apparition what works for you. Also, with regards to really charging for your hours, make sure to keep it sorted out and record the entirety of your time, including thought age, the time it takes you to really make the content (photograph or video), altering time and so forth. Note that there's likewise the typical expense of working together. For instance, if you drive to a plan store to purchase props for your shoot, would you say you are going to charge for that time or for

74

he gas you spent to arrive? This is up to you and your association with the brand. You can bundle it nto your fee or give it to them as a kindness credit and show them on your invoice that you didn't charge for x, y, z).

A few people pass by the way of thinking that time s cash and you have to charge for consistently. Others are more careless on this and simply bundle n basic assignments since they don't have any lesire to be viewed as "nickel and diming." It's truly up to you and what you feel great doing – after all it s your business! One thing to consistently remember is that a few brands dislike paying you constantly so you should gauge the all out time it will take you and afterward quote them a flat fee. ndeed, it might wind up requiring some nvestment than you foreseen, or you may complete somewhat sooner than anticipated however why a company may lean toward a flat fee over an hourly charge is they know precisely what's in store and can budget for the expense.

n case you're charging for costs, make sure to just nclude direct expenses related with each assignment. On the off chance that you did an expert shoot and purchased everybody in your group a Starbucks latte, that was your decision and NOT something we would encourage you to include on your invoice. Here is a model for doing a sponsored post for a sunglass company and you've set your hourly rate at $50:

Sponsored Post Creation: $50/hour
Hours Spent/Or Hours Estimated: 3.5

- 30 minutes researching brand + their rivals
- 1 hour choosing innovative course of photos + all styling
- 45 minutes to shoot item
- 1 hour experiencing photos and altering chooses
- 15 minutes to post and draft inscription

Total: $175

In this case, for micro-influencers, we would suggest providing the brand with the high resolution images you post as well as a few "courtesy photos." So if you provide them with 4 photos total (including the photo you posted), this means the brand paid around $43 per photo (your rate of $175/4 photos). You should then give them the option to purchase additional photos from your roll. If you shot the photos anyway, you might as well try to make some extra cash from them!

OPTION 2: CHARGE BY USING YOUR AVERAGE ENGAGEMENTS PER POST

Some people don't feel comfortable charging an hourly rate. This could be for different reasons but the most common one is that many creatives find it difficult to keep track of every minute they spend on a project. That's why you may want to consider solely charging for your influence and posting on social.

Logically, it makes sense to charge per engagement because on top of an image or video you produce, that is really what the brand is getting in return. It is important to understand that there is an inverse relationship between engagement and follower growth. This means that the more your followers and fans grow, the lower your engagement tends to be. This could be because once you're receiving 30,000+ likes a photo, your audience may not want to give you that "extra like" because they don't think you need it. We know that sounds strange but hey, we don't make the rules. So in terms of pricing yourself for engagement, let's say you receive an average of 3,000 likes a photo and 75 comments per post. The way you can find your average likes is sum up the likes of the last 12 photos you've posted and divide by 12. This math is the same for comments.

Average likes: Total # of likes for last 12 posts / 12
Average comments: Total # of comments for the last 12 posts / 12

Then you would sum up the average likes + average comments to get your average engagement per post.

Average engagement per post = average likes + average comments

You then can establish your fee per engagement (i.e. what is your like, story view or comment worth). Since comments show a higher level of engagement, you can charge a brand more for every REAL COMMENT than a like. Because we like to keep it real, if you are in a comment pod or do any shady business – do yourself a favor and do NOT charge for non-organic comments. This is not an authentic engagement and therefore you shouldn't charge for it. Since you've already spent the time shooting the photo to post, you may as well charge less for a sponsored post and have them purchase additional posts. For example, rather than doing just one post, how about offering them 3 posts with a 30% discount. It's a win-win for everyone because you have to do the upfront work anyway to post just one photo, and they're getting the most bang for their buck with the discount you offered them.

And if you're curious about Insta Story rates, you can charge based on the number of average views you get per story, using the same rate you charge per like and based on the same formula. Remember, brands like to feel like they are receiving more than they bargained for (just like you do) so creating packages with discounts is always a win!

OPTION 3: CHARGE BY USING YOUR CPM RATE

If we need to delve deeper in the marketing scene, we'll fill you in on a typical term – CPM. CPM is the cost for each 1,000 impressions of an advertisement. In any case, why the "M" in CPM? It really represents the Roman Numeral for 1,000. So how would you figure out your CPM Rate? Only 3 simple advances and you're good to go!

Stage 1: You'll need to initially figure out your engagement rate:

(Normal preferences + Average remarks per post/absolute # of followers) * 100

When you have your engagement rate you can utilize the table beneath to perceive the amount you can charge per thousand of followers.

CPM Value Table:
* 1.5-3% engagement = $5 CPM
* 3-5% engagement = $7 CPM
* 5-8% engagement = $10 CPM
* 8% engagement = $15 CPM

Stage 2: Next, you'll have to take the absolute # of followers you have and separate it by 1000.

- If you have 1000 followers, that # will be 10
- If you have 50,000 followers, that # will be 50
- If you have 100,000 followers, that # will be 100
- If you have 250,000 followers, that # will be 250

Contingent upon your engagement level, you will have an alternate CPM esteem.

Stage 3: Plug such information (engagement rate and CPM esteem) into the recipe:

CPM VALUE * (# of followers/1000) = cost per post.

Model: You have an engagement rate of 2.5% and 70,000 followers

$5 * (70,000/1000) = $350 per post.

The Rate for Insta Stories utilizing CPM.

On the off chance that your Insta stories have an alternate engagement rate than your changeless posts, you're going to need to do that equation separately. You'll figure the engagement rate for your stories, and afterward utilize the proper CPM Value and duplicate it times the # of followers/1000, much the same as you did previously. Once more, we generally prescribe making bundles and giving limits. For instance, "1 post will cost X sum, yet in the event that you buy 3 posts, you will get a 30% rebate." And you ought to consistently send the brand a contact sheet of the entirety of the photos you took, that way you can charge for them separately on the off chance that they are keen on buying extra photos from your roll.

Eventually, we realize everybody is at various stages and has various qualities so we can't state there is just a single method to value yourself yet we needed to assist you with excursion by exhibiting various alternatives. Toward the day's end, just you know how you became your following and how genuine your engagement is and when working with brands, you need to feel certain that your evaluating is reasonable.

Earning with Instagram Sponsorship

Influencers receive the respect and praise frpm their audience and receive financial rewards from their sponsors. So it is not surprising that many people strive to reach this level of influence and receive the kudos that accompany the title. In most cases, people by pure luck do not become influential people. They work to build the confidence of their audience and rise in the niche. And as they gain reputation and status, they can see a lucrative Instagram sponsorship prize.

BUILD YOUR REACH AND INFLUENCE

You may think you the photos you post on Instagram are the most eye-catching and attractive images on the net. But they are of little value if nobody sees them. Likewise, you will be of little value to a brand if nobody sees any sponsored posts you make on their behalf. It is easy to be confident and create an attractive Instagram account. But that doesn't make you an influencer. There is one glaring requirement for people to consider you an influencer. You have to actually influence a sizeable number of followers. You need sufficient support from many people to react to your posts. To be an influencer, you need both reach and engagement. You will not receive Instagram sponsorship without these two essential qualities.

INSTAGRAM INFLUENCER SPONSORED POST MONEY CALCULATOR:

The Influencer Marketing Hub can give you a sign of your potential worth as far as Instagram Sponsorship. It adjusts this requirement for followers with the truth that the more followers you have, the harder it is to keep them all locked in. This is one reason that micro-influencers are frequently more successful than superstars. The reach of micro-influencers might be not exactly their celebrity counterparts, yet their followers will in general be considerably more intense supporters.

This makes coherent sense. While you might be somewhat keen on following some celebrity, you presumably give less belief to their suppositions than you do to people you perceive as specialists in a field. Additionally, it is a lot more straightforward for a micro-influencer to speak with an adherent in a two-manner discussion than it is a celebrity. The Instagram Influencer Sponsored Post Money

Calculator perceives this, giving higher commitment weightings to micro-influencers (and even ordinary people) than the purported genius VIPs. You need to adjust the greater reach of bigger accounts with the littler commitment rates.

Regularly, the best influencers online are people with a mid-run following, i.e., certifiable micro-influencers. Thusly, on the off chance that you set yourself with an objective to procure an open to living with Instagram sponsorship, you have to initially set up yourself as a micro-influencer. Brands at first centered around people with high adherent numbers – if not certifiable big names, at any rate the large scale influencers who are geniuses on a particular theme. All the more as of late, in any case, brands have found that reach isn't all that matters. High commitment can be similarly, if not increasingly, basic when finding people who can spread the message.

FOCUS ON A DEDICATED NICHE

The most success Instagrammers concentrate their energies on establishing expertise in a particular niche. A smorgasbord of posts on a range of topics may appear genuine, but they do not build you a devoted audience. The bulk of the people who will follow your Instagram account will do so because they are interested in the images you post and want to hear what you have to say. They share, like, and otherwise interact with your posts if they believe they can trust you.You are effectively building your brand in that niche. Whether you always post images about a particular topic, highlight one specific part of your life, or even just consistently display the same type of picture, you are building your Instagram standing.

In an ideal world, a brand pays those influencers whose followers are a perfect match for their target sales base. So, if you want to earn Instagram sponsorship, you need to build up a following of the type of people who would like the same kinds of products. There is little point having too diverse a range of followers, as this does not advantage potential sponsors.

For example, you might love shoes. You may take note of shoe trends, and possibly wear the latest shoes yourself. In that case, you will want to post images of trendy footwear, so other shoe lovers know they can rely on you to keep them informed if current shoe trends. You want to build up a following of fellow shoe lovers. The first step to gaining Instagram sponsorship is to create your personal brand. What interests you enough to warrant becoming an expert? The vast majority of your posts need to show images related to this topic.

WORK TO A CONSISTENT POSTING SCHEDULE

Your followers will begin to look forward to your posts. You need to build up their trust, so you should set up some form of schedule to emphasize your reliability. Instagram's algorithm also rewards people who post consistently. This is one of the factors that Instagram considers when creating a user's feed. Once brands begin to look at you, they will notice your posting practices, too. They will feed more confident working with somebody who posts regular updates and demonstrates that they can be relied upon. CoSchedule analyzed 14 studies into social sharing and came up with the ultimate number of posts you should make each day on each social network. They found that significant brands share on Instagram 1-2 post per day, sometimes up to 3 times. Adobe recommends even more – up to ten posts per day. Of course, influencers have a more dedicated audience than brands do, so influencers will typically post even more frequently.

DON'T FORGET ENGAGEMENT

Influencers do far more than merely post their favorite pictures on Instagram. They actively engage with their followers. If you find that your followers aren't regularly liking, sharing, and commenting on your posts, then you are doing something wrong. This is the main reason why it is pointless to buy followers. It is unlikely that any followers you gain by this method have any interest in your posts. They are unlikely to even see them. With zero engagement, they are certainly not going to take your advice to buy any sponsored products. Brands are far more likely to sponsor an Instagrammer with a small but active audience than they are somebody with a sizeable unresponsive set of followers.

USE RELEVANT HASHTAGS WITH EVERY POST

Instagram uses extremely good hashtags. In fact, most shared posts on Instagram use more hashtags than you think on other platforms, such as Facebook or Twitter. Instagram allows you to embed up to 30 hashtags in a post. It's usually used by so many people, but it's common to include 10 to 15 hashtags in a message.

A recent change has made it possible for people to follow hashtags. This means that the messages you create contain the appropriate hashtags, even if they have not already been followed. Instagram now rewards posts that include concise and relevant hashtags. But you should definitely stick to the relevant hashtags. Users have the option to select their publication and click on "View this title". If many users do this, Instagram may activate a red flag in its content. This emphasizes that you have to customize your hashtags for each message. You cannot copy and paste a generic set into every message you post.

PREEMPT FUTURE RELATIONSHIPS BY TAGGING BRANDS YOU ADMIRE

One way to become visible to the brand is to mark it in some of your messages. Obviously, you just want to spam it. But every time you publish a publication containing the relevant brand, @ lies in the description of your publication. If you do it often enough, the brand can share your images. This will make your name visible to people using social media accounts. Of course, you have to be strategic here. In many ways, this sounds like an unwanted labor lawsuit. There is no point in tagging in a blurry image that shows a brand with good light. He could even intentionally launch a brand by asking him to share his message in exchange for some of his pictures.

CREATE A PERSONALIZED PACKAGE TO PITCH BRANDS

After gathering a considerable number of devoted followers, you can consider presenting the case for the brand and thus offer services to your influencer. Be sure to adjust your tone to each brand you want to work with. Nothing seems worse than the general tone. Most people start working with small brands before the trucking industry wants to partner with them. Look into some brands in your area and start creating a lot for toddlers. It will be much easier to get started with these companies, though the payments are of course more modest. You can start the process by interacting with brand publications. Use your custom hashtags. Your goal at this stage is simply to gain recognition. By doing this, you can send them a direct message telling them how much you like your brand and suggesting the benefits of possible collaboration. Again, be sure to personalize these messages.

If they reply to your direct messages, you can email them, preferably to your social media manager, if you can find the correct email address. In the next step, you should send them a cover letter informing them of you. This should include your Instagram subscriber information, your niche experience, relevant statistics (or subscriber samples and engagement data), and any notable achievements that have enhanced your reputation as an expert in your field. Finally, in your presentation, you have to tell them why you will make the right decision for your brand, or the benefits you can get.

CONSIDER WORKING WITH A PLATFORM

Another option is to sign up for one of the influencer marketing platforms. You should look for a platform that gives you the ability to become a member, not an algorithm-based platform. The platforms generally accept people who, in their view, share high quality content with decent monitoring (and dedication). Depending on the platform, you might need to wait for your brand to be addressed or you may request a specific campaign.

BE CLEAR ABOUT WHAT A BRAND EXPECTS

If you figure out how to be picked for Instagram sponsorship, it is pivotal that you have clear desires for the brand. You are probably not going to get paid for your work on the off chance that you keep on creating what the brand don't need. You should know the measure of productions paid for by the brand and the kind of content you hope to get ready. Would you be able to make the content yourself or will the brand give the content? On the off chance that this is the last case, you should be a decent counterpart for your followers and sound legitimate. A few brands would like to have a voice in article content, others give you more opportunity. Correspondingly, you should watch that particular hashtags ought to be utilized. Remember that the brand make the principles for sponsored posts. They are probably not going to need to work with you some other time on the off chance that they don't care for the messages you post. It will intently look at the breaks down that show the adequacy of the messages you compose. Finally, remember that Instagram currently anticipates that compelling individuals should submit to the FTC support exposure arrangement. Instagram now has a particular tool that you should utilize each time you distribute a sponsored post.

Ways to Earn Money using Instagram

1. AFFILIATE MARKETING

Affiliate marketing is fundamentally when you promote an item and get paid per sale. You'll frequently observe some bloggers doing this with sidebar flags advancing their partners (affiliates), or even through explicit item roused posts. All things considered, it's very little extraordinary with Instagram. With Instagram, you post appealing pictures featuring their items and drive sales through your affiliate URL (this ought to be given by your affiliate).There are many organizations you can work with here. Here are a few:

• Sharesale: Find organizations you need to work with, pursue their affiliate program, get approved at that point start advancing. In certain projects, it's easier to get approved on the off chance that you have a blog or website.

• Ebates: Refer people that affection bargains and limits, at that point get commission.

• Stylinity: great for design bloggers. At the point when people shop utilizing your link, you'll get commission.

You can put your affiliate URL on your inscriptions or on your profile. You can either utilize bitly.com to abbreviate and modify your affiliate link OR you can connect your blog and Instagram profile so when people buy through your link, you get a sale. It truly couldn't be easier. This kind of marketing is particularly mainstream with clothing on Instagram, as you can post your "OOTD" (outfit of the day) with the affiliate link sending followers to your full outfit subtleties. For those associated with the movement business (or basically those that affection to travel – ahem, we all!), you could attempt to set up and use affiliate marketing when participating in surveys for inns and scenes. Essentially immediate followers to book through your link! It's additionally great for excellence bloggers, as you can welcome people to "shop the look." These techniques are subtler and, in that capacity, more viable than an immediate sales type pitch.

2. MAKE SPONSORED POSTS (FIND SPONSORS!)

Instagram clients with connected followings can win additional cash by making unique sponsored content for brands. More or less, a bit of sponsored content on Instagram is a photograph or video that features an item or a brand. These posts are joined by captions that may incorporate branded hashtags, @mentions, or links. Brands don't normally require a proper brand ambassadorship for makers of sponsored content, however it's not unexpected to for them to tap certain influencers for content over and over. Notwithstanding, it's significant that any brands or products you promote are a solid match for your very own picture on Instagram. The thought is to show off brands that you can by and by get behind, and to show your followers how that brand fits into your way of life.

• TapInfluence is a great tool for Instagram makers who are searching for open doors for sponsored content, and it removes the guesswork from the way toward lining up with brands. You make a profile that portrays you and the idea of your content, and brands who are keen on working with you will welcome you to programs.

• Ifluenz is another simple tool as you can peruse coordinating accessible crusades made by an assortment of brands and legitimately promote the ones you like.

3. SELL YOUR PHOTOS

An undeniable one, unquestionably? Why not utilize Instagram for it sole reason... to showcase your photography? In case you're an expert (or beginner yet sharp!) picture taker, Instagram is a great method to publicize and sell your shots to either people or offices. Add a watermark to your snaps and utilize the captions to list all selling subtleties in a brief way. As usual, make sure that you have a functioning nearness with the goal that the correct kind of accounts are tailing you. Utilize fitting hashtags to pull people towards your shots and get a discussion moving with compelling photography organizations. There are additionally a couple of sites that you can use to really put your Instagram photos available to be purchased, including:

- Twenty20
- Community Foap

4. PROMOTE YOUR BUSINESS, PRODUCTS OR SERVICES

In the event that you maintain your very own business, at that point Instagram needs to hold an essential spot in your marketing lattice. In the event that you sell products, use it to post excellent shots that can't be found on your website. Here are some inventive approaches to promote your products or services:

• Behind the scenes: "In the background" type pictures will in general be colossally prominent – picture lovely carefully assembled cleansers being blessing wrapped, adornments being sorted out or tasty cakes straight out of the stove. It's engaging and adds a specific realness to what you're doing... and people love that.

• Your customers' photos: Linked to this is the utilization of User Generated Content on your account. Get customers to share their pictures of your products and re-gram (download "Repost for Instagram" application to repost your customers' photos). This is a demonstrated fruitful strategy for selling and would make a great expansion to your account. It additionally calls for you to fire up your own unique hashtag which you would then be able to promote to every one of your customers: it's a truly smooth approach to make yourself stand apart from the group. For instance, White Castle requests that their customers use #MyCrave to their photos. Presently when they see them utilizing that hashtag, they can repost (or regram) their photos to their Instagram account.

• Infographics + selective offers. You can likewise showcase your services through Instagram with sweet infographics and selective offers. Utilizing Instagram to include extraordinary offers is likewise a great tool to up your devotee consider it's a reward they won't find anyplace else.

The splendid thing about utilizing Instagram to promote your business is you can get mega inventive with it. Think outside about the container and truly use it furthering your full potential benefit. You're certain to see the sales flying in.

5. SELL YOUR INSTAGRAM ACCOUNT

Had enough of Instagram? Ready to move on? Well, you'll be happy to know that all your hard work hasn't gone to waste. You can actually sell your Instagram account if (for whatever reason) you can no longer manage it. There's a few site that support you with this, two of the best being:

Fame swap
Viral accounts

TOP Instagram Influencers

Now that you know who an Instagram influencer is, the types of influencers available and what they are all about, let's look at who the famous Instagram influencers are these days. Check out this list of the most widely followed online influencers in different business fields to give you an overview of the current Instagram landscape and help you understand what kind of content is mostly consumed in this platform.

INSTAGRAM

With over 302 million followers and counting, perhaps expectedly, Instagram's official page is the most followed. The account is used primarily throughout the platform to showcase various developers that work for them and all about their work life.

CRISTIANO RONALDO

With 169 million followers, Cristiano Ronaldo Soccer player Cristiano Ronaldo made his way to second place on the list of top influencers of

Instagram. He is loved by teeming football fans all over the world who can't get tired of comparing with Messi. Ronaldo's page has majorly soccer-related posts, but on a few occasions he uploads posts about his personal life, including his children, vacation and his mansion

KIM KARDASHIAN WEST

Popular American reality TV personality and socialite Kimberly Kardashian West popularly Known for their reality series on E-network has over time dropped in rankings in. She fell to No. 6 and has over 104 million followers at the moment. She's the Kardashian-Jenner clan's most famous member on Instagram, posting mostly about herself, her family members, and her KKW Beauty brand.

BEYONCÉ

In 2019, on the list of Instagram accounts with the most followers, Beyoncé fell to eighth, with more than 128 million current followers. Her posts have always had a high level of commitment. She shares posts with more than a million likes and many comments per post. Usually, Beyoncé posts pictures of herself or her family. A few years ago, she used her popular Instagram platform to reveal that she was pregnant with Jay-Z husband twins, which made headlines all over the world.

LEO MESSI (LIONEL MESSI)

The Argentine soccer player, Lionel Messi, and best footballer of the year 2019; According to FIFA rankings boasts of over with 120 million followers. He currently holds the ninth place on Instagram rankings. He usually posts about soccer, although he sometimes posts about his family and events.

INFLUENCERS FOR DROPSHIPPING

Who would have thought, right?! Instagram is indeed a market place once you have your niche carved out! There is presently a vast market for dropshipping influencers from Instagram where aspiring entrepreneurs can check through for latest information in the world of drop shipping. These are businessmen who have earned quite a great deal of support in the business world and are focused explicitly on dropshipping business. Here is a list for showing a few of them.

GABRIEL BELTRAN

With more than 73,000 followers, Gabriel Beltran is one of the biggest dropshipping influencers on Instagram. He usually posts business-related motivational content and lifestyle material.

RYAN MELNICK

He is quite an experienced young entrepreneur. He often posts about his life and projects and has over 12,000 followers, and unlike other entrepreneurs, he holds weekly live Q&A sessions, which drives massive engagement from people with mutual interests.

ANTHONY MASTELLONE

Anthony Mastellone (also known to be Tony Mast) is yet another specialist in the Shopify business community, who used Instagram to build his target audience organically. He frequently shares some business tips and inspirational quotes to his more than 7,700 followers. He one of the most information-centred dropshipping influencers of Instagram and loved by his followers.

INSTAGRAM INFLUENCERS RELATED TO FOOD AND NUTRITION

Instagram has given a platform for food influencers all over the world to share their passion for food, nutritional tips, and recipes for various kinds of dishes, with their followers. These influencers range from world-renowned chefs to small-scale café owners, or even people just motivated to share their food journey and experience.

Based on their popularity and because everybody loves food, they have gained a following. For every "foodie" around you, you will discover they have a food influencer they are passionate about. Here we've compiled for you some of the top current Instagram influencers related to food and nutrition.

JAMIE OLIVER

On Instagram, Jamie Oliver British celebrity chef and restaurateur Jamie Oliver has over 7.2 million followers, placing him one of the most popular food influencers. Jamie Oliver is known for his restaurant chain, television shows, and cookbooks. His Instagram is filled with delicious-looking food pictures as well as occasional private images.

NATALIE MORTIMER (THE MODERN PROPER)

The ladies behind The Modern Proper are Natalie Mortimer and Holly Erickson. We are now gaining a lot of attention with more than 150,000 followers after being finalists for Saveur's Best Home-Cooked Food Blog in 2016. They were praised in preparing quick and delicious meals for their modern approach, and that has earned them a place in the hearts of many food lovers all over the world.

TOP PHOTOGRAPHY INFLUENCERS

Instagram Photography's Top Photography Influencers is another category that exploded on Instagram. This makes perfect sense—after all, Instagram is mainly an application for photography.
Here are two top Instagram's photography influencers.

PAUL NICKLEN

Paul Nicklen, with a record 5.4 million followers, is one of Instagram's top photography influencers. A "National Geographic" blogger, Nicklen usually posts photos related to nature and adventure.

CHRIS BURKARD

Burkard is another nature and wildlife photographer who has gained 3.4 million followers on Instagram. His unique, high-quality nature shots attract tens of thousands of likes per post and hundreds of comments.

FASHION INFLUENCERS

Instagram Fashion's top fashion influencers are incredibly popular with Instagram. There are plenty of fashion-focusing Instagram influencers who post pictures and videos about the trending fashion for different seasons of the year. If you are a fashion lover, I'm glad to let you know that you have a plethora of options when it comes to choosing your fashion muse. Here are some of Instagram's top fashion influencers today.

ALEXA CHUNG

Alexa Chung is a vital member of the fashion community of Instagram. She has one of the most followed style pages on the internet with 3.3 million followers. While she has a separate account specifically for her fashion line, there are many fashion-related posts on her account, as well.

Julia Engel is another prominent influencer of Instagram fashion with more than 1.2 million followers. She blogs about Gal Meets Glam, her dress line, and shares other content related to style. Marketing influencers from Instagram is one of the best strategies you can use to create awareness for your brand. As an influencer, you can potentially make thousands overnight without lifting a finger by exploiting the power of influencer marketing on any niche that you may be interested in.

And as you've seen, Instagram has all sorts of influencers from different walks of life. It is time to explore the niche(s) you find interesting, follow them, and even check out what these Instagram Influencers how use various tactics of advertisement to generate leads and traffic for multiple brands all over the world.

Instagram is one of today's most popular social media networks, and it is growing steadily every day, so it is high time you tap into the vast market and create brand name for yourself or at least join a community to learn more. As a brand, If you are not targeting influencer marketing on Instagram, your brand may be lacking a great deal and might not be able to compete with other leading brands in the nearest future, which is why you must ensure you build a successful Instagram account for your brand.

All the tips you need for that are in the preceding pages of this book. Instagram Influencer marketing is one of the easiest ways to spend your marketing budget, and you can be guaranteed to see hundreds or even thousands of people flocking to your product generating quality leads, conversion and an increased ROI.

Do not go yet; One last thing to do

If you enjoyed this book or found it useful I'd be very grateful if you'd post a short review on **Amazon**. Your support really does make a difference and I read all the reviews personally so I can get your feedback and make this book even better.

Thanks again for your support!

CPSIA information can be obtained
at www.ICGtesting.com
Printed in the USA
LVHW082057190621
690650LV00007B/679

9 781914 546747